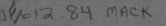

Super Senses

Seeing

Mary Mackill

Heinemann Library
Chicago, Illinois

Printed and bound in China by South China Printing Company Limited
Photo research by Hannah Taylor and Fiona Orbell
Designed by Jo Hinton-Malivoire and bigtop

10 09 08 07 06
10 9 8 7 6 5 4 3 2 1

Library of Congress Cataloging-in-Publication Data
Mackill, Mary.
    Seeing / Mary Mackill.
        p. cm. -- (Super senses)
    ISBN 1-4034-7376-5 (library binding-hardcover) -- ISBN 1-4034-7383-8 (pbk.)
    1. Vision--Juvenile literature. I. Title.
    QP475.7.M33 2006
    612.8'4--dc22

                                              2005018906

Acknowledgments
The publishers would like to thank the following for permission to reproduce photographs:
Alamy Images pp. **5** (Dynamic Graphics Group), **15**, **23d** (Imagestate), **9**; ARDEA p. **19** (C. McDougal); Corbis pp. **16** (royalty free), **21**, **22** (Gavriel Jecan), **4**, **23c** (Randy Faris), **6** (Tom & Dee Ann McCarthy), **18** (William Manning); Digital Vision pp. **14**, **23a**; Getty Images pp. **10**, **13** (Photodisc), **7**, **11**, **12**, **23b** (Stone), **17** (Stone +); Harcourt Education Ltd pp. **20t**, **20b** (Tudor Photography).

Cover photograph reproduced with permission of Superstock/Pixtal.

Every effort has been made to contact copyright holders of any material reproduced in this book. Any omissions will be rectified in subsequent printings if notice is given to the publisher.

Many thanks to the teachers, library media specialists, reading instructors, and educational consultants who have helped develop the Read and Learn/Lee y aprende brand.

Disclaimer
All the Internet addresses (URLs) given in this book were valid at the time of going to press. However, due to the dynamic nature of the Internet, some addresses may have changed, or sites may have changed or ceased to exist since publication. While the author and publishers regret any inconvenience this may cause readers, no responsibility for any such changes can be accepted by either the author or the publishers.

The paper used to print this book comes from sustainable resources.

Contents

What Are My Senses? 4

What Do I Use to See? 6

How Do I See? 8

What Can I See? 10

How Does Seeing Help Me? 12

What Can Help Me See Better? 14

How Can I Take Care of My Eyes? 16

Animals Can See, Too! 18

Test Your Sense of Sight 20

Seeing Is Super! 22

Glossary *23*

Index *24*

Some words are shown in bold, **like this**. You can find out what they mean by looking in the glossary.

What Are My Senses?

You have five **senses**. They help you see, hear, taste, smell, and touch things.

Pretend you are at a fun fair.

What can you see?

Seeing is one of your five senses.

What Do I Use to See?

You use your eyes and brain to see.

Your eyes need light to see objects.

pupil

eye

Each eye has a special hole in the middle. This is called the **pupil**.

The pupil lets light into the eye.

How Do I See?

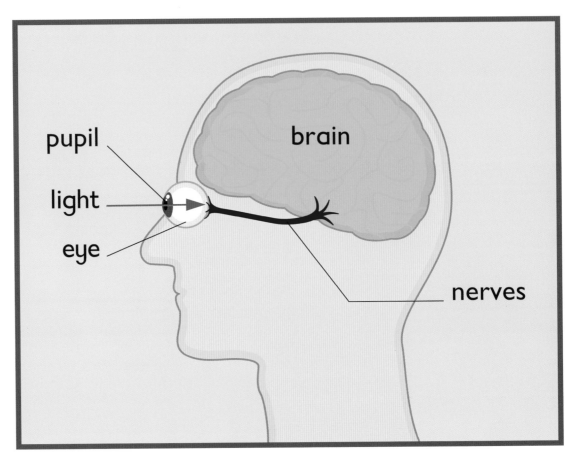

When light comes into your **pupil** it hits some **nerves**.

The nerves send a message to your brain.

Your brain picks up the message.

Your brain would tell you that this ball is coming toward you!

What Can I See?

Your eyes can see lots of colors.

Your eyes can see different shapes and sizes, too.

What shapes can you see here?

How Does Seeing Help Me?

Seeing helps you stay safe.

You can see cars and stay out of their way.

Seeing helps you tell how close something is.

What Can Help Me See Better?

A **magnifying glass** makes small things look bigger.

A **telescope** makes things that are far away look closer.

How Can I Take Care of My Eyes?

Your eyes are important.

Without them, you could not read this book!

Give your eyes lots of rest.

Try not to look at a television screen for too long.

Animals Can See, Too!

Some animals use their **sense** of sight to find food.

Some animals, such as this tiger, can see well in the dark.

Test Your Sense of Sight

This boy can see only a small part of the picture.

When you see all of something, it is easier to tell what it is.

Can you see what this is?

Turn the page to find out.

Seeing Is Super!

Your **sense** of sight:

- tells you what color, shape, and size something is

- warns you if danger is near

- helps you read this book!

Glossary

 **magnifying glass** glass object that makes small things look bigger

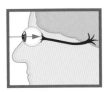 **nerve** part inside your body. Nerves work with the brain to sense things.

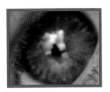 **pupil** hole in the middle of your eye that lets in light

 **sense** something that helps you see, touch, taste, smell, and hear the things around you

 **telescope** large object that makes things that are far away look closer

Index

book 16, 22

brain 6, 8, 9

car 12

colors 10, 22

danger 12, 22

eyes 6, 7, 8

fun fair 4–5

light 6, 7, 8

magnifying glass 14, 23

nerves 8, 23

pupil 7, 8, 23

shapes 11

telescope 15, 23

television 17

tiger 19

Note to Parents and Teachers

Reading for information is an important part of a child's literacy development. Learning begins with a question about something. Help children think of themselves as investigators and researchers by encouraging their questions about the world around them. Each chapter in this book begins with a question. Read the question together. Look at the pictures. Talk about what you think the answer might be. Then read the text to find out if your predictions were correct. Think of other questions you could ask about the topic, and discuss where you might find the answers. Assist children in using the picture glossary and the index to practice new vocabulary and research skills.